AUSTRALIAN
THE CLIMATE CHANGE BOOK

BE INFORMED AND MAKE A DIFFERENCE

Written by Polly Marsden   Illustrated by Chris Nixon

LOTHIAN
Children's Books

This book is about balance.

Can you balance?

I can – but only if everything around me is just right.

I take a deep breath and I hold my arms out wide.

Sometimes I get a little wobbly.

It can be tricky to balance.

This is our home. Planet Earth. Isn't it beautiful?

 here, you'd never know Earth was doing a balancing act of its own.

Earth is made up of many different ecosystems. An ecosystem can be a rainforest or a creek. It can be a mountain, a coral reef or a cold grey sea. Or any other area where living creatures interact with non-living elements, like water or soil.

All ecosystems are connected. And every single thing within them is connected, too, relying on each other to survive. It's a very delicate balance.

Weather has a big impact on Earth's ecosystems.

Over time, ecosystems adapt to predictable patterns of weather.

'Climate' is what we call long-term weather patterns.

Variations in climate normally happen very slowly so our ecosystems have plenty of time to adapt.

But in recent times, climates have started to change too fast.

And ecosystems just can't keep up.

This is what we mean when we talk about 'climate change'.

Why are climates changing faster than ever?
Well, we live in a busy, bustling world ...

... and for a long time, we have used energy sources such as coal, oil and gas to power our world.

Coal, oil and gas are fossil fuels.

Just like dinosaur bones, they are found underground.

In Australia, we burn fossil fuels for power every single day in almost every single way.

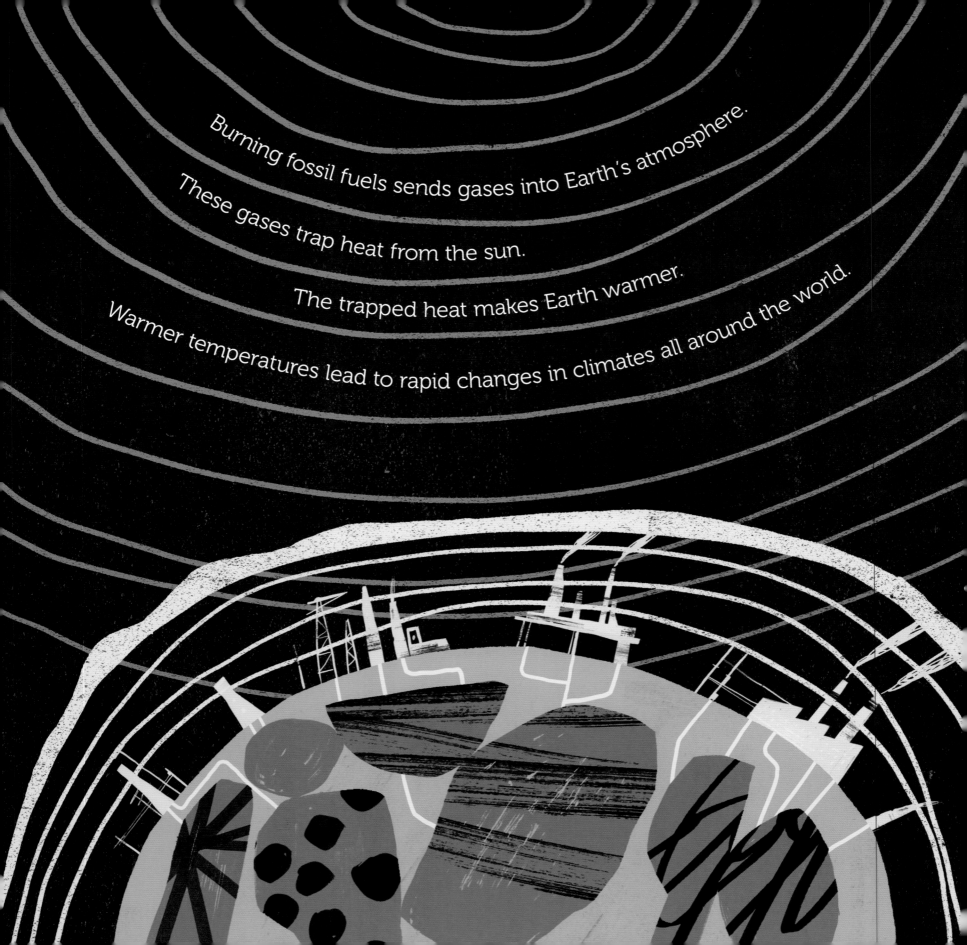

Burning fossil fuels sends gases into Earth's atmosphere.

These gases trap heat from the sun.

The trapped heat makes Earth warmer.

Warmer temperatures lead to rapid changes in climates all around the world.

That doesn't sound good.

It really isn't.

Here's why.

Remember how important balance is to ecosystems?

Climate change upsets that balance.

And when ecosystems are out of balance, the whole natural world is off-balance, too.

Then some VERY worrying things begin to happen.

In Australia, climate change is making
our weather hotter, warming our oceans.

Warmer oceans affect the food and breeding cycles of
marine plants and animals, and lead to coral bleaching.

The Great Barrier Reef is one of the natural
wonders of our world. Warmer oceans are
already harming its coral and fish.

Climate change is making our weather drier, causing droughts and bushfires to be more extreme and less predictable. This affects vital forests such as the Tarkine in Tasmania, the largest expanse of cool temperate rainforest in Australia and one of our most ancient.

Climate change is also causing rising sea levels and bigger storms, with waves, wind and rain wearing away our beaches. This process is called erosion. Erosion threatens the communities who call our coastline home, including the people of the Torres Strait Islands.

Climate change is a crisis for our natural world – and for us.

If we don't reduce the impact of fossil fuels on our environment, then Australia's rarest ecosystems may be lost forever.

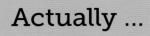

Actually ...

around Australia and the world,
experts are already working hard
to find ways to slow climate change.

They are looking for energy
sources to power our world
that aren't fossil fuels.
Like sun, wind and water!

These sources of energy are
called 'renewables' because
they will never run out.

Some experts are discovering ways to farm plants and animals that are less harmful to the environment.

Psst! Did you know that cows burp methane gas, which also traps heat in our atmosphere? Billions of cow burps = A warming planet

Other experts are educating us about the importance of forests. Because when it comes to slowing climate change,

TREES = SUPERHEROES

Trees take carbon dioxide – one of the gases causing climate change – from the air. They change this gas into the oxygen we breathe.

But it isn't only experts who are fighting climate change.

Millions of ordinary people around the world are making their voices heard so their leaders will listen and take action.

BECAUSE **EVERY BODY** has a role to play in slowing down climate change.

Including you!

Every little action you take to lower the amount
of energy you use will help slow climate change.

SWITCH OFF

Turn off the lights when you leave a room. And, whenever you can, switch off anything else that uses electricity in your home, as the energy to power house appliances comes from fossil fuels.

WALK / RIDE / DANCE

Look for other ways to get about – walk or ride your bike. Petrol is a fossil fuel. By walking, riding (or dancing) through your day you are helping slow down climate change.

EAT LOCAL

When you can, try to eat food grown in your area. Transporting food from far away uses a LOT of fuel. You might even like to try growing your own food – then it doesn't have to travel further than your backyard or balcony!

REPAIR

Fixing things when they are old or broken cuts down on the energy it takes to make them brand new.

Buy products that can be used more than once. When you go out, take your favourite water bottle (and remember to bring it home!). Pass on your toys and clothes to younger friends or charities for others to use when you outgrow them.

RE-USE

RECYCLE

Recycling is when waste is turned into a new product that can be used again. So, next time you take the rubbish out, remember to put recyclables – like plastic bottles or cans – in the recycling bin!

And finally, remember to talk to your friends.
Tell them our planet needs our help. Because when
it comes to balance, even the smallest things can
make a big difference.

To learn about climate change and its effect on Australian wildlife, **World Wildlife Fund Australia** offers important information on its website.

And, to discover practical ways to reduce fossil fuel emissions, check out the work of **Planet Ark**, a leading organisation striving to reduce our impact on the environment.

In recent years, Australian school students have joined worldwide protests to raise awareness of climate change. To find out how to get involved, head to the **School Strike 4 Climate Australia** website.

Remember, talking about climate change might make you feel anxious and worried for the future. That's ok and you're definitely not alone. Thousands of Australians are taking their concerns and turning them into a powerful demand for action. When it comes to tackling climate change there is work being done, but there is still much work to do.

And children, just like you, are leading the way.

A Lothian Children's Book

Published in Australia and New Zealand in 2021
by Hachette Australia
Level 17, 207 Kent Street, Sydney NSW 2000
www.hachettechildrens.com.au

A catalogue record for this
work is available from the
National Library of Australia

ISBN 978 0 7344 2083 1 (hardback)

Front cover design and illustrations by Chris Nixon
Full cover and internal design by Liz Seymour
Printed and bound in China by Toppan Leefung Printing Ltd

CHANGE BOOK

FF

...en you
...henever
...nything
...y in your
...o power
...omes
...s.

REPAIR

Fixing things when they are old or broken cuts down on the energy it takes to make them brand new.

Recycling is when waste is turned into a new product that can be used again. So, next time you take the rubbish out, remember to put recyclables – like plastic bottles or cans – in the recycling bin!

-USE

Look for other ways to get about – walk or ride your bike. Petrol is a fossil fuel. By walking, riding (or dancing) through your day you are helping slow down climate change.

Buy products that can be used more than once. When you go out, take your favourite water bottle (and remember to bring it home!). Pass on your toys and clothes to younger friends or charities for others to use when you outgrow them.

RE

EAT LOCAL

When you can, try to eat food grown in your area. Transporting food from far away uses a LOT of fuel. You might even like to try growing your own food – then it doesn't have to travel further than your backyard or balcony!

LOTHIAN
Children's Books

BE INFO

THE AUSTRALIAN CLIMATE

SWITCH

Turn off the lights w
leave a room. And, w
you can, switch off
else that uses electric
home, as the energy
house appliances
from fossil fu

WALK / RIDE / DANCE